The Dried Flower
Project Book

Joanna Sheen

MEREHURST

Published in 1993 by Merehurst Limited
Ferry House, 51-57 Lacy Road, Putney, London SW15 1PR
Text © copyright Joanna Sheen 1993
Photographs and illustration © copyright Merehurst Limited 1993

Reprinted 1993 , 1995

ISBN 1-85391-111-9

A catalogue record for this book is available from the British Library.

Managing Editor **Heather Dewhurst**
Edited by **Diana Brinton**
Designed by **Lisa Tai**
Photography by **Debbie Patterson** (cover, and pages 4, 5, 8-9, 12-13, 16-17,
20-21, 26-7, 30-31, 36-7, 42-3, 47); all other photography by **Mike Evans**.

Typesetting by **Litho Link Limited**
Colour separation by **Fotographics Ltd UK – Hong Kong**
Printed in Italy by **New Interlitho S.p.A.**

*Merehurst is a leading publisher of craft books and has an excellent range of titles
to suit all levels. Please send to the address above for our free catalogue, stating
the title of this book.*

Contents

Introduction 4

Dried flower basics 6

A basket of garden flowers 8

Nursery ring 12

A kitchen wall basket 16

Golden wedding ring & Table centrepiece 20

Family room arrangement 26

Pot pourri basket & Topiary tree 30

Celebration tree & Flowery picnic hamper 36

Pine mirror & Christmas arrangement 42

Useful tips & Addresses 48

$\mathcal{I}$ntroduction

Beautiful dried flower arrangements add a stunning touch of colour to a dark corner or provide a focal point in a fireplace or on a table. Dried and preserved flowers also last for months, as opposed to days or weeks for fresh flowers, so once you have put some effort into an arrangement you will be able to enjoy the benefits for ages.

The way to get the best value out of dried flowers is to grow and arrange them yourself. If you have a garden in which you can spare a little room, then a couple of varieties of flower can form the basis of a collection that may either be sufficient for simple arrangements or can be supplemented with purchased materials. The section overleaf describes two easy ways of preserving your crop of flowers and leaves.

The projects in this book cover several types of arrangement, and I hope you will enjoy using them and also adapting the designs by varying the materials and colours to suit your individual needs.

Dried flower basics

Many of the arrangements in this book are made with materials that you can grow for yourself, even in a relatively small garden, but there are a few basic materials that you will need to buy. Grey foam is manufactured especially for dried flower arranging, and is usually available in bricks, although it is possible to buy foam spheres, cones and circles. Do not purchase the green foam intended for fresh flower arrangements, as this is too crumbly when dry. Another very useful tool is a hot glue gun, available from craft or DIY stores. The glue is in the form of opaque sticks, which are fed into the back of the gun and heated. The gun is an economical and efficient tool for many projects, and has a wide range of household applications.

DRYING FLOWERS AND FOLIAGE

Two methods of preserving flowers are discussed below – air drying and glycerining. The third method by which flowers can be dried at home is by the use of silica crystals or other dessicants. This can produce very lovely results, but it is a more complicated and expensive process, and none of the arrangements in this book include flowers preserved in dessicants. Pick only the best materials for preserving, and make sure that there is no infestation or disease present.

AIR DRYING

The simplest way of preserving flowers is to hang them up and leave them to dry. The flowers should be hung in small bunches and tied with an elastic band to prevent them dropping on the floor, as their stalks shrink while they are drying. Ideally, flowers should be dried in the dark so that they do not lose any colour before you use them, but if this is not possible, you can compromise: look for a warm but shady place in the house, where you can spare some space to dry your flowers. The drying bunches can look very decorative, but they can also shed bits and pieces so too many in a kitchen can get very messy!

Many flowers are suitable for air drying, especially the everlasting varieties that are advertised on the packet as being ideal for drying. If you look through a seed catalogue or at a display in the garden centre, you are sure to find many ideas for varieties to grow. My favourite flowers to dry are roses. These are simple to dry – just hang up a bunch in a suitable spot; they will dry within a couple of weeks, and many varieties keep their colour very well indeed. Dried roses are very expensive to buy, but whether you grow them or buy them fresh, your home-dried roses will be much cheaper and give you tremendous pleasure.

GLYCERINE

This method does not work for flowers, but it is the only way to preserve many varieties of foliage. Beech is a prime example; this cannot be air dried, but when it is glycerined it makes a very useful foliage that lasts for a tremendously long time. It can also be wiped clean when it has become dusty and re-used many times over. Foliage to be preserved in glycerine should be picked when it is mature – usually middle-to-late summer. Choose only perfect leaves, and do not attempt to preserve branches that are too large, or the leaves at the tips will have wilted before the solution reaches them. Strip the bark off the lower stem; crush the stem to help it to take up the mixture, and make sure that you leave as little time as possible between gathering your materials and putting them in the solution.

Glycerine can be bought from a chemist and you need to mix it with an equal quantity of boiling water. Pour this mixture into a tall slim container until you have a depth of about 7.5cm (3in) and place the stem of the plant you wish to preserve in the mix. The stem will then take up the glycerine and water mixture and you will be able to see the mix progressing up the stem, since with many foliages there is a marked colour change as the glycerine is taken up. The process takes between six days and three weeks, depending on which variety you are preserving. Once the glycerine has reached the tips of the leaves, remove the stem from the vase; if you leave it too long, the stem will take up too much mixture and beads of glycerine will appear on the surface of the leaves, which can lead to a horrible sticky mess and even mildew.

STORING

Once your flowers have been dried or glycerined, you will probably want to store them for some time before using them. Air-dried flowers may be left hanging where they are, if you have the space; if, however, like most of us, you need the space to dry more flowers, your newly-dried, or glycerined, flowers and foliage can be stored in long florists' boxes. (Your local florist will usually be happy to let you have some.) Make sure that you keep the box tightly closed to prevent anything – moisture, children or insects – from harming your stock.

Roses are generally dried, though the heads may also be preserved in dessicants.

A basket of garden flowers

All the wonderful flowers used in this basket can be grown in the garden. Peonies and roses are often expensive to buy, but home-grown specimens can be dried in the house with surprising ease.

✦ basket of garden flowers

Used in this luxurious-looking basket – a lovely reminder of summer to cheer up the winter months – is a collection of hydrangea heads, 15 peonies, two bunches of small cream roses, a bunch of *Atriplex hortensis*, pink and white larkspur (easily grown from seed), and a small bundle of honesty (*Lunaria*) seed heads. The latter are very useful in fresh arrangements when in their early stage, before the seeds are fully developed, and it is a delight to find that they dry so beautifully, retaining their attractive green colour to perfection.

INGREDIENTS

Large basket, with a base measuring approximately 25cm (10in) in diameter

❧

Two blocks of foam

❧

Two pronged foam attachments

❧

Dried flowers and seed heads (see above)

❧

Approximately 1m (3ft) each of pale pink and white ribbon, 2.5cm (1in) wide, with two 0.71mm (22 gauge) florists' wires

1 Glue the pronged attachments to the base of the basket and press the foam blocks on top of them. Cover the foam with hydrangea heads, then add the atriplex and the pink larkspur (trim the stalks – if you leave them too long, the arrangement will be too large and the basket handle will be hidden).

2 Now place the cream or white larkspur throughout the arrangement. The peonies can first be made to look a little larger by steaming them gently over a boiling kettle. Distribute them evenly throughout the arrangement, then add the honesty seed heads in the spaces between the peonies.

3 To finish the arrangement, position the small cream roses at random. Cut each ribbon in two and, taking a length of each colour, form looped bows as shown below, binding the loops with wire, and leaving ends of wire to attach the bows to the arrangement. This is the method used for all the bows in the book.

Forming a ribbon bow

Nursery ring

This ring would make a pretty decoration for a child's bedroom and, as it is hung on the wall, it would be out of harm's way. It could be decorated with rag dolls, as here, or with small teddies or similar toys.

Nursery ring

Twig or cane rings of this type can be purchased from most florists. A small mixed bunch of pink and blue larkspur, a little of either broom bloom or gypsophila (whichever is available), some pink roses and a few sprays of eucalyptus are all the dried materials you will need for this pretty ornament. Small children tend to chew anything they can get hold of, so make sure that it is hung well out of reach, and if you substitute other materials for those used here, check that there is nothing poisonous that might fall to the floor and be eaten.

INGREDIENTS

Twig or cane ring, 20-25cm (8-10in) in diameter

❧

Dried flowers and leaves (see above)

❧

Two small rag dolls, or other small toys

❧

3m (9ft) of matching ribbon, 6mm (¼in) wide for bows (optional), with one 0.71mm (22 gauge) florists' wire for each bow

❧

Glue and glue gun

1 Using a hot glue gun, attach sprays of eucalyptus around two-thirds of the ring, leaving room for the flowers and dolls in the central position. Secure the dolls with plenty of glue, positioning them so that they appear to sit sideways on the ring, rather than staring straight out.

2 Cut the larkspur quite short and glue the stems in place on the ring, mixing blue and pink flowers at random to avoid a regimented effect. Make sure that the larkspur is trimmed sufficiently short – if it is much longer than the eucalyptus this will spoil the finished effect.

3 Still using the glue gun, secure the roses in position one by one, carefully placing them in the remaining gaps in the design. They look attractive either placed in small groups of three or singly. Finally, add a few touches of broom bloom or gypsophila. Whichever you use, it must be cut very short or the ring may look untidy when you have finished. As an optional finishing touch, you might like to add a ribbon bow with streamers (see page 11 for the basic method, but form streamers as well as loops).

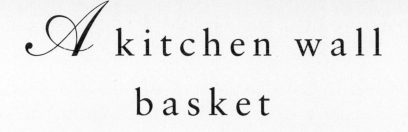

A kitchen wall basket

An attractive collection of herbs, spices and preserved bread rolls makes a marvellous conversation piece in a kitchen. It is arranged in a flat-backed basket so that it can hang out of the way of the work surfaces.

$\mathscr{A}$ kitchen wall basket

The bread used in this arrangement is preserved by drying it slowly in the bottom of a cool oven for several hours until it feels very light. Once the rolls have cooled, spray them all over with a matt varnish to protect them from insects. The dried materials that are added to the bread and cinnamon to make up this unusual wall basket are marjoram, oregano and natural wheat, together with atriplex. When choosing a position for your wall basket, make sure that it is away from the main cooking area – excessive dampness can cause mildew.

INGREDIENTS

A flat-backed wall basket, with a pouch measuring approximately 20cm × 15cm (8in × 6in) at the base

❧

Half a block of foam

❧

Five each of bread rolls, cinnamon sticks, and very heavy gauge florists' wires

❧

Dried materials (see above)

❧

1.5m (4ft 6in) of terracotta ribbon, 2.5cm (1in) wide, for bows (optional), with two 0.71mm (22 gauge) florists' wires

1 Glue the foam into the basket and cover it with hydrangea heads. Spread the wheat throughout the basket, using most of a large bunch, to give good colour and to fill the basket. Use the wheat fairly short or you will obscure most of the basket once the arrangement is finished.

2 Push a thick wire into each of the bread rolls and, if necessary, glue the wires into the rolls. Next, place the rolls evenly through the arrangement. Add some cinnamon sticks by pushing the ends into the foam. Use a small bunch of atriplex to help to fill the basket and to add touches of stronger colour.

3 Finish the basket by adding the marjoram and oregano – both of which not only contribute wonderful colours to the basket, but a lovely herbal scent as well. Terracotta ribbons can be formed into two bows, one at each side of the basket (see page 11).

Golden wedding ring & Table centrepiece

Either of these, or both together, would make a delightful gift for a golden wedding celebration. These arrangements are very versatile and, with minor changes in colour, could be adapted to suit numerous occasions.

Golden wedding ring

Unusual golden wedding presents are hard to find, and this ring will please on two counts – it is beautiful to look at, and you will have the additional pleasure of making it yourself. The roses used here were the variety 'Calypso', but any golden shade, or even a cream, would be suitable. Two bunches of the roses were combined with one bunch of *Achillea filipendula*, one of cream helichrysums and glycerined beech leaves. The dried materials are attached with a hot glue gun, in the same way as those used for the Nursery ring (see page 12).

Ingredients

Dark twig ring, 30-35cm (12-14in) in diameter

❧

Dried materials (see above)

❧

1m (3ft) each of cream and gold ribbon, 2.5cm (1in) wide, for bows (optional), with two 0.71mm (22 gauge) florists' wires

❧

Glue and glue gun

1 Using a hot glue gun, attach some sprigs of beech leaves in position, covering about two-thirds of the ring. Make loops with tails from both colours of ribbon; wire them (see page 11), and then glue them just left of centre, on the base of the ring.

2 Add the achillea flowers, cutting off the stems so that you are attaching just the main head of each flower. Place them evenly around the ring – if you cluster them too close together there will not be enough room for the roses and helichrysum heads.

3 Next, attach the helichrysum heads, again distributing them in a random fashion around the ring, without crowding any too close together. When these are in place, attach the roses one at a time, making sure that each is firmly glued in place. The roses can be placed in small groups or individually.

$\mathcal{T}$able centrepiece

Although the arrangement shown here has gold candles in it, you could easily substitute another colour, such as ivory or yellow. This would be an ideal centrepiece for a golden wedding celebration, but it could equally well be used for Christmas or any other festive occasion. Never leave the arrangement unattended when the candles are lit; like all dried materials, those used here – eucalyptus, white *Achillea ptarmica*, cream peonies, yellow 'Calypso' roses and *Nigella orientalis* seed heads – are all highly inflammable.

INGREDIENTS

Flat cork base, an oval measuring approximately 22.5cm × 17.5cm (9in × 7in)

Small piece of foam and pronged foam attachment

Two 22.5cm (9in) gold candles and candle holders

Dried materials (see above)

2m (6ft) of gold ribbon, 12mm (½in) wide, for bows (optional), with four 0.71mm (22 gauge) florists' wires

1 Glue the pronged foam attachment to the cork base and push the foam onto it. Trim 2.5cm (1in) from the candle and insert the two holders and candles into the foam. Cover the foam with lengths of eucalyptus, taking care to ensure that none of the foam will show. Try to follow the shape of the base, maintaining the oval.

2 Trim the peonies very short and place these at the centre of the arrangement, spacing them carefully so that they are not all crowded at one side – remember that the arrangement will be viewed from all sides and at a slightly downwards angle when in use. (It is often better to make this type of arrangement from a seated position.) After you have positioned the peonies, distribute the Nigella orientalis *seed heads throughout the arrangement.*

3 Finally, trim the stems of the 'Calypso' roses and add them to the arrangement. Also add small clumps of Achillea ptarmica. *Again, distribute both the roses and the achillea evenly throughout the design. Cut the ribbon into four equal pieces and, taking a length for each bow, make four ribbon bows (see page 11) and decorate each side with these.*

Family room arrangement

This attractive arrangement uses various cones, reeds, grasses and dried flowers to achieve a finished effect which is a subtle blend of cream and sepia tones that would suit many different styles of decor.

Family room arrangement

A large and very stylish arrangement, this combines hydrangea heads, ten cream peonies and the same number of proteas, salignum cones with foliage, and one bunch each of bell reed, foxtail millet and polypogon grass. The materials used are generous in size and the finished effect should be lavish, so you will need to find a basket with a high handle, like the one shown here. Failing that, it would be preferable to have no handle at all, and let the reeds and grasses give the essential height to this elegant arrangement.

Ingredients

Large basket, with a base measuring approximately 20cm (8in) in diameter

❧

One and a half blocks of foam

❧

Pronged foam attachment

❧

Dried materials (see above)

❧

0.71mm (22 gauge) florists' wires

❧

1m (3ft) of cream ribbon, 2.5cm (1in) wide (optional)

1 Glue the pronged foam attachment to the base of the basket and impale the foam block on it. Cut the half block in two and glue the pieces to each side of the main block to help fill the basket evenly. Cover the foam with hydrangea heads, then position the foxtail millet and salignum cones.

2 Place the cream peonies in position, setting five to each side of the basket handle. Do the same with the proteas, to make sure that the larger ingredients are evenly dispersed. As you work, look at the arrangement from different angles, to check for balance.

3 Arrange the bell reed and the grass into small clumps of five or six heads and wire them together (without this, they would be dwarfed by the larger materials). Scatter the clumps throughout the arrangement. Form the ribbon into four bows (see page 11), and place two bows at each side of the basket.

Pot pourri basket
&
Topiary tree

*If you make this pretty tree for yourself, you are likely to be
inundated with requests from friends to make one for them. The
charming pot pourri basket would be an equally welcome gift.*

Pot pourri basket

Pot pourri is a delightful gift in itself, but how much more elegant it is when presented in a charming basket, decorated with dried flowers! The basket is lined with polythene, to prevent the pot pourri from slipping through the gaps. If your basket is not ready-lined, you could line it with paper or fabric. The dried materials comprise pale pink roses, pink-peach statice, pink larkspur, green oregano, marjoram and dyed green statice (*Goniolimon tataricum* var. *angustifolium*, often known as *Statice dumosa*).

INGREDIENTS

*Shallow basket, lined, with
a base measuring
20cm (8in) square*

Dried flowers (see above)

*0.71mm (22 gauge) florists'
wires*

*2m (6ft) of toning ribbon,
1.5cm (¾in) wide, and the
same of transparent ribbon*

Glue and glue gun

Pot pourri to fill the basket

1 Using the two ribbons together, make two wired bows with the ribbons (see page 11) and glue them to the base of the handles at each side of the basket. Then glue the pink-peach and green statice along the sides of the basket, around the bows.

2 At this stage, you may decide to continue the design around the entire basket, if you have sufficient materials. The next flower to be added is the pink larkspur. Take care not to keep the larkspur spikes too long, or the final effect will be spidery rather than compact. When the statice and larkspur have been fixed in place, add the marjoram, wiring it into small clumps and attaching these to the basket.

3 Finish by filling in the remaining gaps between flowers with the pale pink rosebuds and a small number of tiny wired bunches of green oregano flowers. When the decorations are finished, fill the basket with pot pourri, soaps, chocolates, or whatever else you may have in mind. This basic design is very quick to make and the colours can, of course, be adapted to the filling; a basket for a lemon-scented pot pourri, for example, might be more appropriately edged with yellow statice and cream or deep purple rosebuds.

Topiary tree

These miniature trees make a very attractive decoration for a hall, living room or bedroom. The dried materials used here were hydrangea heads, *Achillea millefolium* 'Cerise Queen', pink larkspur, dark pink helichrysums and *Nigella orientalis* seed heads. The dried helichrysums can be bought ready-wired or you can wire them yourself when they are fresh, and dry them wired. For the cement, you can use ordinary building cement, fast-drying cement or plaster-of-Paris.

INGREDIENTS

12.5cm (5in) terracotta flower pot

⁂

Small quantity of cement, and a straight stick, approximately 40cm (16in) high

⁂

Foam ball, 9cm (4½in) in diameter, and small pieces of foam block

⁂

Dried materials (see above)

⁂

0.71mm (22 gauge) florists' wires or glue and glue gun

⁂

1m (3ft) each of two shades of pink ribbon, 12mm (½in) wide

1 If the pot has a hole in the base, cover this with a piece of cardboard. Mix the cement and fill two-thirds of the pot. Once the mixture has stiffened a little, stand the stick in the centre. Leave to dry for two to three days, then impale the ball on the stick. Glue small pieces of foam to the cement, bringing the level to the top of the pot.

2 Cover both the ball and the foam at the base of the stick with hydrangea heads, broken down into smaller pieces.

3 Push in pieces of Achillea *'Cerise Queen' until you have achieved a good covering of both the ball and the base. Next, using fairly short pieces to avoid a straggly effect, add the pink larkspur. Take care to work in the round, stepping back regularly to take a quick look at the overall effect from a distance.*

4 Finally, put in the helichrysums. They can be glued in position, but in this case they were wired. To wire a helichrysum, remove the stem, then push the wire up from the back, near the centre of the flower; make a small hook at the upper end of the wire, and pull the wire back down, securing the hook in the centre of the flower. When you have distributed the helichrysums around the tree, add a good number of Nigella orientalis *seed heads, to give a contrast in both shape and colour. Make two wired bows with the ribbon (see page 11), leaving long legs of wire to be pushed well into the foam ball.*

Celebration tree
&
Flowery picnic hamper

*These two projects show the versatility of dried flowers –
the tree is a lavish arrangement which would do credit to a
major occasion, such as a wedding, while the hamper has a
quiet rustic charm that would look attractive in virtually
any room.*

Celebration tree

This is a very large version of the tree shown on page 34. It takes a long time to make and you will need to take care to cover the ball well. It is also expensive, but once it is made it will last a long time and give many months – or even years – of pleasure. In addition to the lining of hydrangea heads, the ingredients for this tree included eucalyptus, dyed green statice (*Goniolimon tataricum* var. *angustifolium*, often known as *Statice dumosa*), box foliage, cream peonies, *Achillea ptarmica*, cream helichrysum heads and poppy seed heads.

INGREDIENTS

25cm (10in) flower pot or similar base

❧

Broom handle, and cement

❧

Foam ball, 20cm (8in) in diameter, and two foam blocks

❧

Dried materials (see above)

❧

5.5m (18ft) of cream ribbon, 4cm (1½in) wide, with three 0.71mm (22 gauge) florists' wires

❧

Glue and glue gun

1 Cover any hole in the base with card then fill with cement to 5cm (2in) below the rim. When the cement begins to set, insert the stick, supporting it upright. Leave to dry for three to four days, then impale the ball on the end of the stick. Slice the foam blocks and pack them around the base, level with the rim of the pot.

2 Cover the foam ball and the foam at the base with an even layer of hydrangea heads.

3 Add the green statice in small bunches and the other foliage, in this case eucalyptus and an exotic box. Make sure that the entire ball is evenly covered with greenery.

4 Add the poppy heads and also the cream peonies. To make the peony blooms a little larger and fuller, steam them over a boiling kettle. This softens the flowers slightly so that you can carefully shape them in your hands to make the blooms larger. Finally, add the achillea and glue in the helichrysum heads. The ribbons can be made into three large loops and tails, wired (see page 11), and then inserted at the same angle as the broom handle. The same flowers and foliage are then added to the base of the tree.

Flowery picnic hamper

This small picnic hamper would look equally at home in the hall, living room or a bedroom. It has been filled with an unsophisticated selection of materials that are reminiscent of fields in summer. The dried materials seen here are dyed green statice (*Goniolimon tataricum* var. *angustifolium*, often known as *Statice dumosa*), and one bunch each of natural poppy heads, white everlasting daisies (*Helipterum roseum*, also sold as *Acroclinium roseum*), yellow helichrysums, natural wheat and pale and dark blue larkspur. You may, however, wish to vary the flowers and grasses somewhat to suit your own decor while retaining the overall effect.

INGREDIENTS

Picnic-style basket with a base measuring approximately 20cm × 15cm (8in × 6in)

❧

Half a block of foam

❧

Pronged foam attachment

❧

Dried materials (see above)

❧

1m (3ft) each of cream and blue ribbon, 2.5cm (1in) wide, with two 0.71mm (22 gauge) florists' wires

1 *Glue the pronged attachment to the base of the basket and push the foam onto it. Cover the foam with green statice. Add the poppy heads, distributing them evenly at each side of the basket.*

2 *Add in the wheat, ensuring that it is longer than the statice, but still in proportion to the basket. Use most or all of the bunch – plenty of wheat will help to give an attractive green effect to the arrangement. Next, place the darker blue larkspur in position. Again, make sure there is an equal amount at each side of the basket or one side of the arrangement will look darker than the other.*

3 *Insert the pale blue larkspur at the same height as the darker blue. Use plenty, to give a good strong blue to the arrangement. Put the white daisies in next, scattering them in small clumps throughout the arrangement. Lastly, place the yellow helichrysums in position. These may either be wired (see page 35, step 4) or attached with a hot glue gun. Wire two ribbon bows (see page 11), using both colours together, and attach a bow to each side of the basket.*

Hall mirror & Christmas arrangement

One of the joys of dried flowers is that they last so long, and both the decorations shown here will still be looking good long after the festive season has come and gone.

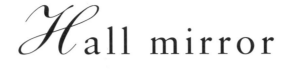Hall mirror

The dried materials featured here comprise eucalyptus leaves, 'Mercedes' roses, larch cones, *Nigella damascena* seed heads, and statice (*Goniolimon tataricum* var. *angustifolium*). They were attached with a hot glue gun – you could use a cold adhesive, but it would be much more difficult. If you feel that the red roses and the cones used here look too Christmassy for a permanent feature like a mirror, you could easily substitute another variety of rose and use seed heads in place of the cones. Your local picture framer will make a mirror for you if you cannot find a suitable one.

INGREDIENTS

30cm × 25cm (12in × 10in) pine-framed mirror

≥১

Dried materials (see above)

≥১

Glue and glue gun

≥১

Cardboard and clips or blu-tack (optional – see step 1)

1 Clean the mirror and place it the correct way up. The materials were glued directly to the mirror shown here. If you do not want to make a permanent feature, you could cut cardboard carrying strips about 17.5cm (7in) long and the depth of your frame and attach these to the mirror with clips or blu-tack. Glue the statice and eucalyptus in place.

2 Next, place the red roses in position. It is a good idea to lay them all on the mirror and make sure that you are happy with the design before you glue them permanently in situ.

3 Add the larch cones and the nigella seed heads. Try to get a good balance between the top and bottom of the mirror so that you do not get the feeling that one is considerably heavier than the other. Take great care when using the gun not to let any glue drip onto the mirror – it can take a long time to clean mistakes away.

Christmas arrangement

This basket of dried flowers will add a festive touch to a coffee table or create a welcoming atmosphere in the hallway. The dried materials used were statice (*Goniolimon tataricum* var. *angustifolium*), *Achillea millefolium* 'Cerise Queen', gilded salignum foliage, gilded bell reed and gilded wheat, eucalyptus, pine cones and two bunches of red 'Mercedes' roses.

INGREDIENTS

Dark rustic basket, with a base measuring approximately 15cm (6in) in diameter

Block of foam

Pronged foam attachment

Dried materials (see above)

0.71mm (22 gauge) florists' wires

3m (9ft) of tartan ribbon, 2.5cm (1in) wide

1 Glue the foam in the basket; cover it with statice, and then add the eucalyptus. Wire each cone: bend a wire in a 'U' shape; wrap it round the bottom section, and twist the ends together. Insert about five each side of the handle.

2 Add the gilded ingredients, and finally the achillea and the roses. Finish with ribbon loops (see page 11), one at each side of the arrangement.

Useful tips & Addresses

For dried flower courses, pot pourri oils and some ingredients:

Joanna Sheen Limited
PO Box 52
Newton Abbot
Devon TQ12 4QH

For dried flowers:

The Hop Shop
Castle Farm
Shoreham
Sevenoaks
Kent TN14 7UB

The majority of the flowers and other materials used in this book were air dried, the exception being the beech leaves, which were glycerined. Air drying is extremely simple, as explained on pages 6-7, but if you have been inspired by the foregoing arrangements to harvest and dry your own materials, there are a few extra hints and tips that may be useful.

Eucalyptus The silvery-green leaves of the young growth on a eucalyptus tree are particularly useful in arrangements. Ensure that you have plenty of young growth to harvest by a continual pruning process. Cut in mid-season and either air-dry or (for a darker colour) glycerine.

Helichrysums These very popular everlasting flowers are often picked far too late. Harvest them when the outer petals are just starting to open, but the middle is still tightly closed, as they

will continue to open after they have been cut. They can then be wired through the centre of the flower or hung in bunches.

Hydrangeas These must not be picked too early or they will crumple up and fail to keep their colour. Wait until the flowers on the bush are quite papery, then pick them and arrange them loosely in grey foam until they are completely dry.

Nigella orientalis This is very similar to *Nigella damascena*, but the seed heads of the former are larger and spikier, and therefore I generally prefer to use them in arrangements.